I0503609

STOCK INVESTING SECRETS

Everything you need
to know about making
money with stocks.

Justin Harrison

FOREWORD

Most people I know lose money with stocks and it's no surprise why. Most of them are doing day trading and the rest are sold into trying the latest trick to get rich quick.

In Stock Investing Secrets, Justin takes this extremely complicated and technical subject and does a complete 360 by showing you that there is an easy way to invest in stocks.

In simple terms, he explains what the stock market is, the history of the stock market and what it has evolved into today.

If you ever did a Google search about analyzing a stock then you know how overwhelming the information can be. However, in a few pages, Justin shows you how to analyze a stock, what makes it a good investment and how to set up your trading account in less than 10 minutes.

I never thought it would be possible to compress all this information into that few pages but Justin managed to do just that.

Justin has this incredible gift to take a complicated subject and teach it to you in a language that a child can understand.

After reading this book you will never want to go down the rabbit hole again when it comes to stock investing. I know that's how I felt after reading it and I know you will feel the same.

David Bester

INDEX

INTRODUCTION

I nvesting in the stock market can be one of the riskiest investments you ever make, or it can be one of the most financially rewarding.

It all depends on your knowledge of how the stock market works, how to choose stocks and your personal investment strategy.

This book aims to cut through all the technical jargon, get straight to the point and provide you with both the knowledge and actionable points to enable you to make your first stock purchase and beyond.

You are going to learn the exact strategies I have used to grow my personal wealth using the stock market, and discover the unknown strategies used by some of the world's best investors to consistently choose winning stocks that deliver consistent returns year after year.

Best of all I am going to show you a way to purchase stocks directly, without any fees, without any technical knowledge and without having to do hours of boring technical analysis.

If you have not already done so, I highly suggest you get copies of my first two books "$MONEYSECRET" and "COMPOUND INTEREST SECRETS" as the two books form part of the larger knowledge foundation that I will be referring to throughout this book.

At the end of this book, you will have a firm understanding of how the stock market works, what your investment options are, and how to go about choosing stocks to invest into.

As with any advice you receive in life, I urge you to keep an open mind and follow a process of logic before you start your investment journey. So if you are ready to learn, lets jump right in.

WHAT IS THE STOCK MARKET?

The stock market is where investors connect to **buy** and **sell** investments, most commonly, stocks, which are shares of ownership in a public company.

The concept behind how the stock market works is pretty simple. Operating much like an auction house, the stock market enables **buyers** and **sellers** to negotiate prices and make trades.

The stock market works through a network of exchanges such as the New York Stock Exchange (NYSE) or the Nasdaq. Companies list shares of their stock on an exchange and investors then purchase those shares, which allows the company to raise money to grow its business.

Investors can then buy and sell these stocks among themselves, and the exchange tracks the supply and demand of each listed stock.

Historically, stock trades took place in a physical marketplace. These days however the stock market works electronically through the internet.

The key role of every stock market, from New York to Hong Kong is connecting buyers with sellers to trade under an agreed-upon set of rules.

HISTORY OF THE STOCK MARKET

The first stock markets didn't arrive until the 1500s. However, there were plenty of early examples of markets which were similar to stock markets.

In the 1100s France had a system where courtiers de change managed agricultural debts throughout the country on behalf of banks. This can be seen as the first major example of "brokerage" and they effectively traded debts.

Later on, the merchants of Venice were credited with trading government securities, and soon after, bankers in the nearby Italian cities of Pisa and Florence also began trading government securities.

THE WORLD'S FIRST STOCK MARKETS (WITHOUT STOCKS)

The world's first stock markets are generally linked back to Belgium. Flanders, and Rotterdam in the

Netherlands all of which hosted their own "stock" market systems in the 1400's and 1500's.

All of these early stock markets had one thing missing: stocks. Although the infrastructure and institutions resembled today's stock markets, nobody was actually trading shares of a company.

Instead, the markets dealt with the affairs of government, businesses, and individual debt. The system and organization was similar, although the actual properties being traded were different.

THE WORLD'S FIRST PUBLICLY TRADED COMPANY

The East India Company is widely recognized as the world's first publicly traded company, and there was one simple reason why it became the first publicly traded company: **risk**.

Simply put, sailing to the far corners of the planet was too risky for any single company. When the East Indies was first discovered to be a haven of riches and trade opportunities, explorers sailed there in droves.

Unfortunately, few of these voyages ever made it home. Ships were lost, fortunes were squandered, and **financiers realized they had to do something to**

mitigate that risk.

As a result, a unique corporation was formed in 1600 called "Governor and Company of Merchants of London trading with the East Indies". This was the famous East India Company and it was the first company to use a limited liability formula.

Investors realized that putting all their eggs into one basket was not a smart way to approach investment in the East Indies trading.

Let's say that a ship returning from the East Indies had a 33% chance of being seized by pirates. Instead of investing in one voyage and risking the loss of all invested money, investors could purchase shares in multiple companies. Even if one ship was lost out of 3 or 4 invested companies, the investor would still make a profit.

The formula proved to be very successful and within a decade, similar charters had been granted to other businesses throughout England, France, Belgium, and the Netherlands.

In 1602, the Dutch East India Company officially became the world's first publicly traded company when it released shares of the company on the Amsterdam Stock Exchange. Stocks were issued to investors and each investor was entitled to a fixed percentage of East India Company's profits.

SELLING STOCKS IN COFFEE SHOPS

Long before investors yelled across trade floors and threw order forms into the air, they conducted their business in coffee shops.

Before long, somebody realized that the entire business world would be more efficient if somebody made a dedicated marketplace where people could trade stocks without having to order a coffee or yell across a crowded café. And that's where the idea for the original "stock market" of today originated from.

THE FIRST STOCK MARKET BUBBLE

Nobody really understood the importance of the stock market in those early days. People realized it was powerful and valuable, but nobody truly understood exactly what it would become.

The early days of the stock market was like the Wild West. Businesses would open up overnight and issue stocks in some crazy new venture, raising massive sums of capital before a single ship had ever left the harbour.

There was absolutely no regulation and very few ways to distinguish legitimate companies from illegitimate companies. As a result, the bubble quickly burst. Companies stopped paying dividends to investors and the government of England banned the issuing of shares until 1825.

THE FIRST STOCK EXCHANGE

Despite the ban on issuing shares, the London Stock Exchange was officially formed in 1801. Since companies were not allowed to issue shares until 1825, this was an extremely limited exchange.

This prevented the London Stock Exchange from creating a true global superpower, and that's why the creation of the New York Stock Exchange (NYSE) in 1817 was such an important moment in history.

The NYSE has traded stocks since its very first day. Contrary to what some may think, the NYSE wasn't the first stock exchange in the United States. However, the NYSE soon became the most powerful stock exchange due its positioning at the centre of U.S. trade and economics.

The London Stock Exchange was the main stock market for Europe, while the New York Stock Exchange was the main exchange for America and the world

MODERN STOCK MARKETS

Today, virtually every country in the world has its own stock market. Even war-torn countries like Iraq have their own stock markets.

Every day, trillions of dollars are traded on stock markets around the world and they're truly the engine of the capitalist world.

After dominating the world economy for nearly three centuries, the New York Stock Exchange (NYSE) faced it's first legitimate challenger in the 1970's when the NASDAQ was formed.

The NASDAQ, instead of having a physical location is held entirely on a network of computers and all trades are performed electronically.

And in 2007 the NYSE merged with Euronext to create the first transatlantic stock exchange pushing us further into the digital era.

DOW JONES AND OTHER MAJOR INDICES

Stock market indexes around the world are powerful indicators for global and country-specific economies, and the Dow Jones Industrial Average is arguably the most important index in the world.

The Dow Jones Industrial Average was one of several indices first created by Wall Street Journal editor Charles Dow and is made up of 30 publicly-owned large companies involved in heavy industry, which is why it's called the "Industrial" Average.

Today, many of the companies listed on the index have little to do with heavy industry. Companies are added and removed from the index over time to reflect their influence on the U.S. economy.

GLOBAL IMPACT

Today, there are many stock exchanges worldwide, each supplying the capital necessary to support industry growth. Without these vital funds, many revolutionary ideas would never become a reality, nor would fundamental improvements be made to existing products.

In addition, the stock market creates personal wealth and financial stability through private investment. This allows individuals to fund their retirement and other ventures.

The stock market has truly become an opportunity for everyone.

WHY DO COMPANIES GO PUBLIC?

B efore we talk about investing in stocks, it is important to understand why a company would go public and take on shareholders money in the first place.

Going public and offering stock in an initial public offering (IPO) represents a milestone for most privately owned companies. A large number of reasons exist for a company to decide to go public, such as obtaining financing outside of the banking system etc.

Taking a company public makes raising a lot of capital quickly much easier than traditional methods, reduces the overall cost of capital and spreads the risk of ownership among a large group of shareholders.

Spreading the risk of ownership is especially important when a company grows, with the original shareholders wanting to cash in some of their profits while still retaining a percentage of the company.

One of the biggest advantages for a company to have its shares publicly traded is having their stock listed on a stock exchange.

ADVANTAGES FOR A COMPANY HAVING LISTED STOCK

In addition to the prestige a company gets when their stock is listed on a stock exchange, other advantages for the company include:

- The company is able to very quickly raise additional funds through the issuing more stock at anytime.

- Stock and stock options programs can be offered to potential employees, making the company attractive to top talent.

- Companies have additional leverage when obtaining loans from financial institutions if they are listed.

- Having a company's stock listed on an exchange is excellent market exposure often attracting the attention of mutual and hedge funds, market makers and institutional traders.

- The filing and registration fee for most major exchanges includes a form of complimentary advertising, and the company will benefit from some indirect advertising.

- Having a listing on a stock exchange also affords the company increased credibility with the public, having the company indirectly endorsed through having their stock traded on the exchange is good for a companies brand equity.

A WORD OF CAUTION

Today most markets are heavily regulated and there is a lot of good work being done to make sure that only legitimate companies list on the stock market for most of the reasons stated above.

Unfortunately, as will always be the case when it comes to people and money, there will always be a few unscrupulous and greedy people out there trying to make a fast buck and that's where the final reason comes in.

It's called the "exit strategy" and it works a little like this:

A company will offer an IPO after having been initially funded with private venture capital. Unsurprisingly these companies usually do not have a very strong trading history. Once the IPO goes live and the money has been raised on the open stock market, the original owners cash in their shares and leave the small investors holding the bag when the shares become worthless.

This is why it's absolutely critical to do your homework when investing into any company and buying stock. You need to know why they are listing and what they motives are!

INVESTING VS DAY TRADING

When most people think about investing in the stock market chances are it is along the lines of day trading. Additionally if you do a simple google search around investing in the stock market, chances are you will be presented with what is commonly known as day trading programs.

Sadly day trading has created a massive false impression of the stock market, and in my personal opinion has been responsible for a massive erosion of personal wealth amongst smaller investors hoping to get in on the market.

SO WHAT IS DAY TRADING?

Day traders, much like long term stock investors are also seeking profit in the stock market, but they pursue that goal in a very different way.

Day traders typically jump in and out of stocks

within weeks, days, or even minutes, with the aim of short-term profits. They mostly focus on a stock's technical factors rather than a company's long-term prospects.

What matters to day traders is which direction the stock will move next, and how the day trader can profit from that move in the immediate term.

The most significant difference however is that most day traders don't actually invest in the underlying stocks themselves, since they are trading in and out of these stocks so quickly. Instead they trade what is known as a contract for difference (CFD) which is a very fancy way of saying they "place a bet" on what the price will do.

What makes day trading through CFD's so risky and also potentially so lucrative is that trading platforms allow investors to leverage their "bets" on the price movements often by a factor of 20, since investors are only "betting" on the price movements and not actually purchasing the underlying stocks.

The reality however is that 78% of day traders lose all of their invested capital to the trading platforms, and since not a single cent gets invested in an actual stock it is the trading platforms that are walking away with the money.

So when you understand this, you understand that

day trading is no different than going to a casino and placing a bet in the hands of a third party such as the casino hosting the game. You never truly had a stake in the game at all.

HOW IS INVESTING DIFFERENT TO DAY TRADING?

One of the key differences between investing in stock and day trading stock is that when you invest in stock you actually buy the underlying stock. This means you own an actual share of whatever company stocks you purchase.

Additionally stock investors have a longer-term outlook. They think in terms of years and often hold stocks through the market's ups and downs. Timing is the big difference between traders and investors, and this means the focus also differs dramatically.

Investors study a company's potential for long-term growth and value, but traders mainly take advantage of small mispricings in the market, once the temporary mispricing is corrected, a trader will move on to find the next temporary mispricing, while investors will hold for the long term.

Most investors are more focused on earning dividends (share of profit) from their stock rather than the immediate gain in share price. For this reason it's practically impossible to compare day trading to investing in stocks, not to mention that day trading is a lot like gambling rather than actually investing.

IMPORTANT TERMINOLOGY

Annual Report

This is a report prepared by a company that contains information about the company, from its cash flow to its management strategy. When you read an annual report, you're judging the company's solvency and financial situation.

Averaging Down

When an investor buys more of a stock as the price goes down, this reduces the average purchase price of the investors shares. An investor might use this strategy if he believes that the stock price will rebound later.

Bear Market

This is trading talk for the stock market being in a downward trend, or a period of falling stock prices. If a stock price plummets, it's very bearish.

Bull Market

When the stock market as a whole is in a prolonged

period of increasing stock prices, its known as a bull market or bullish.

Blue Chip Stocks

The stocks behind large, industry-leading companies. They offer a stable record of significant dividend payments and have a reputation for sound management. The expression is thought to have been derived from blue gambling chips, which is the highest denomination of chips used in casinos.

Bid

The bid is the amount of money a trader is willing to pay per share for a given stock. It's balanced against the asking price, which is what a seller wants per share of that same stock.

Dividend

A portion of a company's earnings that is paid to shareholders, on a quarterly or annual basis. Note that not all companies pay dividends.

Exchange

A place in which investments are traded. The most well-known exchanges in the United States are the New York Stock Exchange (NYSE) and the Nasdaq.Execution

When an order to buy or sell has been completed, the trader has executed the transaction.

High

A high refers to a market milestone in which a stock or index reaches a greater price point than previously. Record highs can signal that a stock or index has never reached the current price point, but there are also time-constrained highs, such as 30-day highs.

Index

A benchmark that is used as a reference marker for traders and portfolio managers. A 10 percent return may sound good, but if the market index returned 12 percent, then you didn't do very well since you could have just invested in an index fund and saved time by not trading frequently.

Initial Public Offering (IPO)

An IPO is the first sale or offering of stock by a company to the public. It happens when a company decides to go public rather than remain solely owned by private or inside investors. The Securities Exchange Commission (SEC) has strict rules that companies must follow before issuing an IPO.

Leverage

I'm not a fan of leverage, but it's good for you to know this stock market term. When you use leverage, you borrow shares in a stock from your broker with the goal of increasing your profit. If you borrow shares and sell them at a higher price point, you return the shares and keep the difference. It's a dangerous game that I urge you to avoid playing.

Margin

A margin account lets a person borrow money (take out a loan, essentially) from a broker to purchase an investment. The difference between the amount of the loan and the price of the stocks is called the margin. Trading on margin can be dangerous because if you're wrong about the direction in which the stock will go, you can lose significant cash.

Moving Average

A stock's average price-per-share during a specific period of time is called its moving average. Some common time frames to study in terms of a stock's moving average include 50 and 200 day moving averages.

Order

An investor's bid to buy or sell a certain amount of stock or option contracts constitutes an order. You have to put an order in to buy or sell shares.

Portfolio

A collection of investments owned by an investor makes up his or her portfolio. You can have as few as one stock in a portfolio, but you can also own an infinite amount of stocks or other securities.

Rally

A rapid increase in the general price level of the market or of the price of a stock is known as a rally. Depending on the overall environment, it might be called a bull rally or a bear rally.

Stop Loss

Stop-loss orders are designed to limit an investor's loss on a position in a security and are different from stop-limit orders. When a stock falls below the stop price the order becomes a market order and it executes at the next available price. For example, a trader may buy a stock and places a stop-loss order 10% below the purchase price. Should the stock drop, the stop-loss order would be activated, and the stock would be sold as a market order.

Spread

This is the difference between the bid and the ask prices of a stock, or the amount for which someone is willing to buy it and the amount for which someone is willing to sell it. For instance, if a trader is willing to trade X stock for $10 and a buyer is willing to pay $9 for it, the spread is $1.

Stock Symbol

A stock symbol is a one to four-character alphabetic root symbol that represents a publicly traded company on a stock exchange. Apple's stock symbol is AAPL, while Walmart's is WMT.

Volatility

The price movements of a stock or the stock market as a whole. Highly volatile stocks are those with extreme daily up and down movements and wide intraday trading ranges.

Volume

The number of shares of stock traded during a particular time period, normally measured in average daily trading volume. Volume can also mean the number of shares you purchase of a given stock. For instance, buying 2,000 shares of a company is a higher-volume purchase than buying 20 shares.

Yield

This refers to the return on an investment that is received from the payment of a dividend. This is determined by dividing the annual dividend amount by the price paid for the stock. If you bought stock X for $40 per share and it pays a $1.00-per-year dividend, you have a "yield" of 2.5 percent.

HOW TO EVALUATE A STOCK

E valuating a stock can be as simple or as complex as you wish to make it. In this chapter I will provide the most common ways to evaluate a stock.

Typically most people will fall into one of two categories when evaluating stocks, the over analytical types who spend hours on research and those who jump in with little or no research. Hopefully, this chapter will provide a comfortable bridge between the two extremes.

The Price-to-Book Ratio (P/B)

The price to book (P/B) value is the quickest way to look at the overall value of a company. This is a surface scan of the value before you dig deeper.

The P/B ratio represents the value of the company if it is torn up and sold today. This is useful to know because many companies in mature industries falter in terms of growth, but can still be a good value based on their assets. The book value usually includes equipment, buildings, land and anything else that can be sold, including stock holdings and bonds.

With purely financial firms, the book value can fluctuate with the market as these stocks tend to have a portfolio of assets that goes up and down in value.

Industrial companies tend to have a book value based more in physical assets, which depreciate year over year according to accounting rules.

In either case, a low P/B ratio can protect you, but only if it's accurate. This means you have to look deeper into the actual assets making up the P/B ratio.

The P/B value is calculated as follows: The **book value** of the company divided by the number of **outstanding shares** in the market. Then the current **share price** divided by the number between the book value and outstanding shares. This gives you your P/B Ratio.

So as an example, let's say a company's book value when you look at the balance sheet is $1,000,000 and there are 100,000 outstanding shares and the shares are valued at $20 per share. The P/B ratio would be calculated as follows: $1,000,000 / 100,000 = 10 $20/10 = P/B Ratio of 2

The P/B ratio of 2 means that the stock is twice as expensive as the assets could be sold for. So basically investors or market sentiment is that the company is worth twice as much as its book value.

Generally speaking a P/B value under 1 can indicate a highly undervalued stock, and a stock with a very high P/B ratio could indicate significant positive investor confidence, which in both cases warrant a deeper look.

Price-to-Earnings Ratio (P/E)

The price to earnings (P/E) ratio is possibly one of the most important ratios to look at when scruitizing a stock, and the reason for this is that a P/E ratio can be thought of as how long a stock will take to pay back your investment if there is no change in the business.

As an example, a stock trading at $20 per share with earnings of $2 per share has a P/E ratio of 10 (20 divided by 2), which is seen as meaning that you'll make your money back in 10 years if nothing changes to that stock.

Many long term investors try to find companies with higher P/E ratios that they think will become progressively more profitable each year and therefore lower the P/E ratio over time (shortening the payoff period significantly).

Additionally, many companies that have inflated stock prices that do not have the earnings to back up that stock price will eventually fall back down and push up the overall P/E ratio.

It is always good to compare P/E ratios among companies in similar industries to get an understanding of what similar market conditions are like.

THE PRICE TO EARNINGS GROWTH RATIO (PEG)

Since the P/E ratio on its own isn't enough to determine the value of a stock, many investors use the price to earnings growth ratio (PEG) aswell. Instead of only looking at the price and earnings, the PEG ratio incorporates the historical growth rate of the company's earnings.

The PEG ratio is calculated by taking the P/E ratio of a company and dividing it by the annual growth rate of its earnings. The lower the value of your PEG ratio, the better the deal you're getting.

For example, let's say you're analyzing a stock that is trading with a P/E ratio of 16. Suppose the company's earnings per share (EPS) have been and will continue to grow at 15% per year. By taking the P/E ratio (16) and dividing it by the growth rate (15), the PEG ratio is calculated as 1.07.

By comparing two stocks using the PEG ratio, you can see how much you're paying for growth in each case. A PEG of 1 means you're breaking even if growth continues as it has in the past.

A PEG of 2 means you're paying twice as much for projected growth when compared to a stock with a PEG of 1. This is speculative because there is no guarantee that growth will continue as it has in the past.

The P/E ratio is a snapshot of where a company is and the PEG ratio is a graph plotting where it has been. Armed with this information, an investor has to decide whether it is likely to continue in that direction, but at least he/she is basing that decision on some historical facts.

As always it is always good to compare PEG ratios among companies in similar industries to get an understanding of what similar market conditions are like.

Dividend Yield

It's always nice to have a back-up when a stock's growth falters. This is why dividend-paying stocks are attractive to many investors, even when stock prices drop, you get a paycheck and for true investors this is the holy grail of investing in the stock market.

The dividend yield shows how much of a payday you're getting for your money. By dividing the stock's annual dividend by the stock's price, you get a percentage.

You can think of that percentage as the interest on your money, with the additional chance at growth through the appreciation of the stock.

Although simple on paper, there are some things to watch for with the dividend yield. Inconsistent dividends or suspended payments in the past mean that the dividend yield can't always be counted on.

Like water, dividends can ebb and flow, so knowing which way the tide is going, like whether dividend payments have increased yearly, it is essential to making the decision to buy.

Dividends also vary by industry, with utilities and some banks typically paying a lot whereas tech firms invest almost all their earnings back into the company to fuel growth.

Not all companies pay dividends, so it is important to know which ones do and which ones don't. Most solid companies pay a quarterly dividend that is somewhat predictable to investors. These companies typically pay a regular quarterly dividend around the same times every year.

For a company that has a stock price that is trending upward, it will need to raise its dividend payout in order to maintain its dividend yield.

For example. if a stock goes up by 50%, but does not raise its dividend, its yield will drop significantly lowering the attractiveness of the stock.

Here is an example of how to calculate a dividend yield. If stock X had a share price of $50 and an annualized dividend of $1.00 per hare, its yield would be 2%, which is calculated as follows **$1.00 / $50 = .02 * 100 = 2%**

Dividend yields will vary with interest rates and general market conditions, but typically a yield of 4 to 6 percent is considered quite good. A lower yield may not be enough justification for investors to buy a stock just for the dividend income alone.

However, a higher yield may indicate that the dividend is not safe and may be cut in the future. So it's always good to be conservative and aim for stocks with a yield of between 3 to 8 percent.

NON TECHNICAL EVALUATION

There literally is no limit to the amount of analytical ratios and equations to evaluate a stock.

In fact there is an entire industry built around technical trading that studies graphs, data patterns and trends, none of which have proven any more effective than good old common sense, which is why my final stock assessment method is full of old school logic.

A company is only as good as the people running it. So make sure you read up on them, make sure you know who they are and what they stand for.

Are they part of the business DNA, or are they just a bunch of number crunchers.

Look at the products and services you use, and ask yourself if you would use these products and services. If you do not, why would you invest in a company like that?

Google around and see what the sentiment around the company and its management and its staff is like. The web has given us all the power to look into every major company these days and see exactly what's going on.

The bottom line is this, don't just sit in front of a computer screen and press "buy", do some gut feel research as if you were handing over cash in the real world and I promise you that you will find the value stocks to invest into.

WHERE AND HOW TO BUY AND SELL STOCKS

There are basically two ways to buy and sell stock stocks, you can either trade through a broker or directly online through a trading platform.

TRADING THROUGH A BROKER:

Many banks and investment houses like Charles Schwab and Citigroup offer brokerage services allowing you to set up an account, and deposit cash into brokerage account which then becomes your trading account.

Once you open an account you have the option of having a discretionary account or non discretionary account.

A discretionary account allows the broker to execute trades on your behalf without your consent. Many older investors choose this option due to their lack of market knowledge.

Additionally clients using brokers may opt for a non discretionary account, which means that the client would need to consent to every trade. This is normally used more by institutions that are trading through a brokerage.

Brokers typically earn a commission for every trade executed, this normally amounts to several cents per share for every trade.

If you would prefer to use a broker a good place to start would be to ask your bank for their brokerage division, however it would be a good idea to shop around and compare fees as broker fees can vary quite a bit.

Also consider very carefully the track record of the broker, even if he/she is with a large institution, and make sure to evaluate their trading history before deciding on giving them a discretionary mandate.

TRADING THROUGH ONLINE PLATFORMS

If you are prepared to do the research, if you have the discipline to avoid trying to get rich quick, and you have the patience to check in with your stocks daily, trading through online platforms is the way to go.

Not only is it cheaper, it's quicker to execute trades, often more secure and you have faster access to your money should you need it. However be warned for all the upsides to online stock buying there are massive downsides.

Firstly, most of the stock buying platforms are promoting "day trading" and this means that you could inadvertently land up buying leveraged CFD's.

Secondly most of the online trading platforms tend to "gamify" the buying of stocks detaching investors from the reality of the market.

However if you follow my advice in the next chapter on buying your first stock, which will be done through an online platform then you will be just fine.

What I love about online trading platforms is the availability and access to information, especially being able to view and monitor your portfolio on a daily basis, and being connected to what's happening in the market.

I have broker accounts, and believe me, being able to see my money daily as opposed to having to call my broker for statements is like driving a car versus walking. You just cannot compare the two, not to mention the opportunities you find by constantly checking in on the market.

BUYING YOUR FIRST STOCK

There are many fantastic online stock buying platforms and you are welcome to check all of them out, however most of them deal in CFD's, which means that you are placing "bets" on the price movement of the stock and not investing in the actual stock.

For this reason, I am a big fan of **eToro** not only do they allow you to trade CFD's if you want but you can also buy the actual stocks instead, which is what the focus of this course is.

I highly recommend you head over to **eToro** and create an account, get setup and verified which can take a day or two because they need screen all new account applications for security reasons. Once that's done, you can make a small deposit via credit card, bank transfer or even paypal to get started.

Choose your stock

Once you are logged into your **eToro** account, select

the stock you want to buy by clicking on the trade button next to the stock. This will open up a window with options to purchase the stock.

Make sure you pay close attention to the next step as this is critical to making sure you buy the actual stock and not the leveraged CFD.

Change the leverage to 1

On this step you get to choose how much stock you want to purchase, but most importantly at the bottom you get to choose if you buy a leveraged (CFD) or the underlying stock.

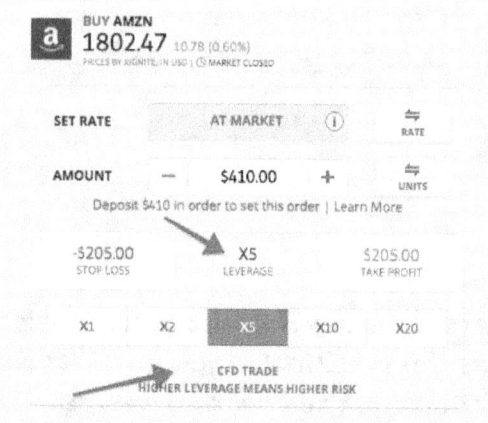

Make sure you change the leverage to X1 to buy the underlying stock. This means you will own real shares and you will pay zero commission in your purchase and be entitled to dividends if the company pays dividends.

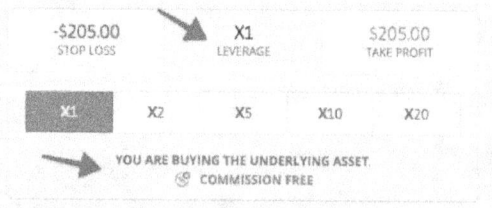

Additionally it is my advice to remove the automatic stop loss and automatic take profit limits when you invest in real shares because when you invest in real shares you should be there for the long term and be willing to ride through various market conditions.

If the system triggers automatic buy and sell signals this could seriously mess with your plans in your portfolio, and it is always best to manually execute these trades as and when the need arises.

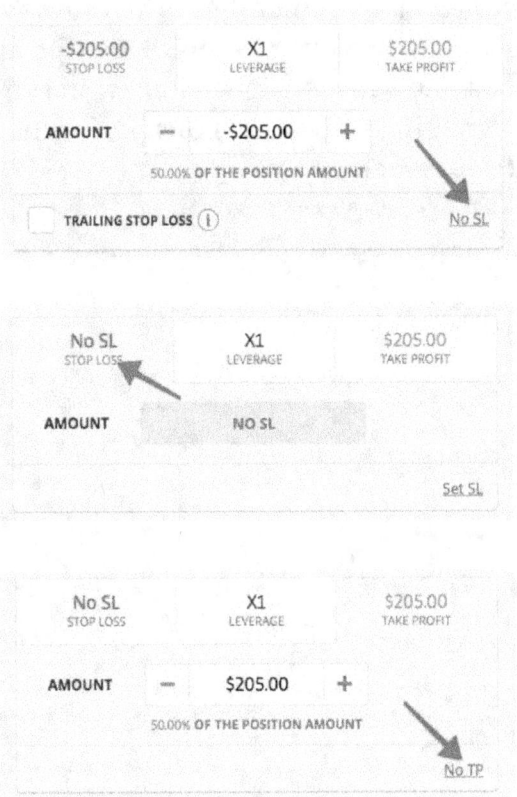

It is important to remember when removing the automatic stop loss and automatic take profit limits that you are now responsible for checking your portfolio and making active decisions about when to buy and sell your stocks.

STOCK INVESTING STRATEGIES

There are literally thousands of stock investment strategies, many of them work, many of them don't. However over the years I have found that one thing beats them all and that is consistency.

If you have read my first two books "$MONEYSECRET" and "COMPOUND INTEREST SECRETS" you will understand that there is no shortcut to wealth creation and the single biggest reason 78% of retail investors lose in the stock market is because they come looking for instant profits and chase unrealistic margins, and that usually ends in disaster.

If I could show you a way to get a 20% consistent return on your money with very little risk, you would basically be doubling your initial investment within 3.6 years and if you worked it out over a 10 year period and applied to logic I presented in the COMPOUND INTEREST SECRETS course I 100%

guarantee you will retire comfortably if not rich.

Just for a matter of illustration if you put $50,000 into the market for 10 years at a 20% annual rate of return it will be worth **$363,412.75**

With that said the benefits of finding stable long term investments are pretty obvious. Sure its alluring to hear about the guy who bought Mcirosoft shares at $2.00 and is now a millionaire, but those realities are hit and miss, when it comes to your future, you need a plan that is less of a gamble and more of a sure thing.

It has been my personal experience and the same for many of the most successful investors I know that the simpler your investment strategy the better you will perform long term.

Here is the step by step template I follow when deciding on which stocks to invest my hard earned money into, I highly suggest you use it.

SIMPLE INVESTMENT STRATEGIES

- Only look at companies whose products you use daily, or have a deep understanding of. This insight alone is priceless.

- Only look at companies that have been around for a long time and have an established track record both financially and ethically.

- Only look at companies that have a track record of successful successive management hand overs.

- Only look at companies that are multinational. Companies that do not operate globally pose a higher risk of becoming obsolete and are at risk of operating in single markets and single currencies.

- Only look at companies that have established brands, assets and unique IP that gives them a clear market edge.

- Only look at companies that consistently pay out dividends to their shareholders and have a consistent dividend yield.

Once you have shortlisted a few stocks based on the list above then it would be good to look at the P/B, P/E, and PEG ratios as well as studying the dividend yields.

Based on this information, you should be making a decision based on solid fundamentals rather than sentiment or pure technical analysis.

Combining these simple strategies along with the basic technical analysis to finding stocks to invest into is the definitive key to long term success and growth in the stock market.

INVESTMENT SUMMARY

- Know that most companies list publicly to raise capital mainly so they can **share risk** amongst investors (aside from all the other reasons stated in this book), so when you are buying shares, know that you are essentially **buying risk.**

- Know the difference between day trading (buying CFD's) and investing in stocks for the long term and make sure you mitigate risk by always buying the underlying asset (stocks) when building your portfolio

- Don't rely purely on technical analysis of stocks when purchasing, make sure to do some fundamental research on companies, just like you would if you were buying a company in the real world.

- Stop chasing unrealistic profit margins, instead focus on slow and steady growth in fixed and steady stocks that will provide an above average yield, which is better than what you could get in the banks etc.

- Always take a long term view when investing in the stock market and be prepared to go through the market cycles (both the ups and downs) and avoid the temptation to jump in and out of stocks too quickly.

- Focus on finding stocks that have a history of consistent dividend yields, this way you are not only buying the future appreciation value of the stock, but you are buying into a share of the companies profits.

- Don't be tempted to take profits, instead take your dividends and profits and put them back into the market consistently, this will not only grow your portfolio but will have a long term compounding affect on your wealth and overall net worth.

- When buying single stock investments always try and hedge your investments. For example if you buy Apple Stock, you should also buy some Microsoft stock as a hedge against any possible negative market movements on the apple stock and visa versa.

- While mutual funds and index funds may be

alluring because all of the work has already been done for you, often these funds attract higher fees and dont always outperform single stocks, for this reason I always advise new investors to first learn to invest with single stocks before investing across mutual funds and index funds.

- Signup for a free account with eToro start watching other investors, use the demo account, and get to understand how the market works before you make a live stock investment.

- Never let emotion get in the way of any decision you make when it comes to buying and selling stocks. Look at the fundamentals, study the core P/B, P/E, PEG ratios and dividend yields and make your decisions purely based on that.

- Remember there are thousands of investment strategies, and just because something is more complex does not mean it will give you a better result. Stick to the old school logic and you will see steady and profitable long term returns.

- Investing in the stock market can be risky if you don't do your research, however if you do your research and you watch the markets its one of the best ways to increase your personal wealth.

CLOSING THOUGHTS

I nvesting in the stock market can be an extremely complex subject, this is the reason so many people don't invest, and for those that do a large percentage get conned out of their money because it's easy to confuse new investors.

I truly hope that this book has opened your eyes to the reality and possibility of investing in the stock market. I have very purposely kept this book as simple as possible to get you to making your first stock purchase in as few steps as possible with as much background understanding as possible.

As you leave this book and head over to google in search of more information and engage in discussions with friends, I have no doubt the temptation to over complicate things will come. This is where I urge you to **KEEP THINGS SIMPLE** and stick to the basics within this guide.

I have built my fortune on simplicity, as has people like Warren Buffet, Henry Ford, Bill Gates, Steve Jobs and many of my personal friends who are extremely wealthy. You don't need to be super smart, you just need to be super persistent and super consistent.

The more you **earn**, the more you should **save**, and then the more you should **invest,** and then just let **compound interest** do the rest.

~ Acknowledgements ~

I would like to thank my business partners, Dale Maxwell, Laura Palmeri, David Bester and Chris du Toit who have held down the fort while I took the time to write this book. Without their support and input, this book would never have become a reality.

I would especially like to thank Laura for her critical eye and constant proofreading, which helps a dyslexic, barely literate guy like myself seem capable of writing something worth reading.

I would also like to extend an extra-special thank you to my wife Andrea who as always offers constant constructive criticism and input, and unwavering support. Thank you for always making sure I have no distractions when I write and for your total commitment. I could not have asked for a better partner.

Last but not least, I would like to give an extra heartfelt thank you to David for sharing my vision and helping bring these ideas to life. Your work ethic and dedication to Global Money Academy is inspiring.

First printing, 2019.

Team 6 Investment Holdings Ltd.

5th Floor, Ritter House,
Wickhams Clay II,
Road Town, Tortola
British Virgin Islands

www.globalmoneyacademy.com